Let Us Bring Order

Verleiz Lattimore, MBA, MED

ISBN: 0988263203
ISBN-13: 978-0-9882632-0-8

Dedicated To Alvin Lattimore

Only You!

Table Of Contents

ACKNOWLEDGMENTS

Thanks to my mom who is still leading and guiding, you will always be my number one hero.

To my husband, my Alvin, thanks for the support and help, love you to life.

To my Morgan, Tee- Tee does it all to see you do better.

Also my big brother, thanks for believing in me even when you didn't see the plan.

~*Introduction*~

What goes up has once been down; we should never fear failure because it is only feedback. It is not who you are when you arrive it is what you do when you are on the journey. Success is in the process of creating the success and being willing to take the risks.

Many people never get passed the idea because they never make the first step. Fear of the first step paralyzes individuals into failure. How can you know what you are capable of if you don't try? You have thankfully made a first step by purchasing this book. Congratulations! You get in life what you invest in and you are a great investment. All you need is to invest your thoughts into your true potential and success.

I believe I can help you met your goals because I have come to understand the model of success. I have come to a place in life where success is magnetized to me the same way I know I can show you to magnetize success to you. I believe in your ability to change your life into the one you have imagined therefore I want to give you the keys I know will insure you the success you desire. I know that reading this book will be an eye opener for you and after you do so you will begin to feel the world open up to you. In addition, by going to www.LetUsBringOrder.com you will gain access to more tools, resources and the complete Let Us Bring Order system that will invoke your success.

If I can share but one secret to success with you while we take this journey together I can offer you the keys to freeing your mind to accomplish anything your heart desires. I can assure you this book will renew your mind as I offer you these tested truths, so that I can do as life does and give to the giver.

I want to take this journey with you because I believe in sharing what I have learned. At the age of thirty-one I find that just the right information and the right amount of risk can help you to move forward. I took a risk when I went to college for Fashion Design and acquired an Associate's Degree. I took another risk when I went on to get my Bachelor's in Education and Psychology. I turned around and took yet three more risks when I went from my MBA in Marketing and Project Management, to my MED in Curriculum Design and Instructional Technology and then another Bachelor's in Metaphysics. All of these risks paid off in the end because they gave me specialized knowledge that has help to build my businesses and ideas. It may not make sense to some but all my risks make sense to my plans and goals, which help to create www.RennyConsulting.com.

I found what I loved in life and pursued a means to make it all work together for my success. You too can find what it is you want from life the most and make great things happen for you. It is not about what the world labels you as; it is what you will label yourself as. You have the God given right to create a great life for you and your family.

In these pages you will find your road map to success on your own terms. You will make the links with what will catapult you into your greatest potential. Life is like clay you have to mold the experience you desire. You want change you have to create it, and you are more than able to do so.

This book will help you to once again find your voice, as you begin to feel alive and in control again. You will see yourself for the great, successful person you are. Let's begin this journey to the new you together. I want you to decide now whether you are truly ready for change. Do you know you want better? Are you ready to find out how to get better?

Are you ready to be set free? If you have said yes to all of these questions I want you to begin to make a promise to yourself. Write in the space below, **YES I CAN!!!!!** And sign your name.

_____

(Signed here for your success)
You have just promised yourself success. We shall find the hidden treasure within you. Let Us Bring Order!

So The Journey Begins

~*Whose Life is This?*~

Chapter One

One of the first steps to moving forward in your life is to ask yourself, *who's life is this?* Are you living the life you want or a life planned by someone else? When you look in the mirror of your life are you seeing something or someone you like? Many of us wander the earth for years following the blueprint that someone else has drawn, never fulfilling the actions that are in the blueprints that are given to us for our own dreams. Hearing the voice of another and not listening to the voice of our own experience.

So once again I ask, *who's life is this?* Are you

living the life you want or living the life that someone has planned for you? If you are seeking this book you are probably living someone else's plan however you have realized you are ready to live the life planned by you. So first, it is time for you to sit down and find out what is in this plan of yours. Who do you want to be in life, what do you want to see manifest? What is it you feel you want to accomplish? What is your inner voice saying to you?

The reason planning is so important is that it literally directs your path, without a vision the people parish. If you feel like you are vanishing, then you have failed to focus in on the vision for your life. Goals are the key. I always advise my clients to start by listing ten goals. These are the goals that line up your plan; they are the foundation of your blueprint. You need to make these goals solid and treat them as anchors for your life. You should also be mindful of the goals you are setting because these are truly those things that will carry you to the next level. So list things that hold meaning and truly hold your hearts desires.

Most clients want the new home, the husband or wife, or the successful financial life. These are goals that will motive positive outcomes. Change comes through and from motivation. What will motive you? What goals will cause you to get in gear and really work at the increase in your happiness? These are the goals you start with no matter how large they are, the bigger the dream the more motivation. You see greatness is waiting dormant in you, waiting for you to plan for it to come out. It is not waiting for your best friend to say it is there or for your parents to give it direction. ***It is waiting for you!*** You have to live your own life, you have to give yourself permission to move in the things that life has for you.

Why limit yourself? Tap into those goals that take you into your dreams. If you are working in an office right now in your dream occupation and you have two supervisors above you, make it your business to see yourself in the top position. That should be your goal. No matter if you are not educated enough or if you are not outgoing enough. These are things you can change, and these things change by first setting the goals to change them. The larger the goals the more you can change.

Many of us fear change. Let me first state that fear is totally useless. Fear will kill the dream, the vision and the goals. Face your fear first! The best way to face fear is by saying to yourself, "this is my life, and I am not going to take it anymore." Then take the first action that will lead you to the goal you desire. Success takes willingness and the ability to take risks. Taking action puts you in the state of believing you can do. You have now stepped around fear into the position to decide that you are going to hold the vision you have your heart set on.

Change is also challenging to some, but change will create the new you, the new life. Change is necessary; you will not be the same person you are today when you create the life you truly want. If the you, you are today could make this all happen you would not need to read about getting to where you want. Be it a small change or a very big change, you will change. Change is nothing to fear, I look back on the old me and smile today because I love the new me; the growth, the strength, the creation of opportunity. I've taken the idea of a makeover to the next level. I now look, feel and sound like the part I want to play in life.

Having a plan and setting goals will create a happier, healthier you. You will not have time to worry, only time to see your goals through, time to move toward the new improved life you have mapped out. Having a road map also helps when the Naysayers and the protagonist show up. Those who begin to notice the change and decide it is their duty to tell you, you are going to fail. Come to the table with your head held high. "This is my plan and

I am sticking to it." So what goals 1 through 5 are a long shot and they can't see you making them happen. Well guess what, I may not know you half as well as they do but I think you can make every single last one of your goals happen and I think you should try thinking just a bit bigger. Texas is definitely on to something with "bigger is better."

You have to learn to live life for you. It is your world, now you create it. If you have always wanted to open a coffee shop and you make a mean cup of Joe, **HELLO**! Start the goals you need to set to live the life of a coffee shop owner. You have to find the life within your mind that creates the most joy. Little do you know the universe is waiting for you to find this harmony. Your health, wealth and happiness are tied to one thing, your true desire to live your dreams. Successful men and women love what they do and guess what. They made plans to get there and are making plans in order to stay there. You can go to www.letusbringorder.com where I have provided tools and resources I want to share with you to help you make these plans and accomplish your dreams!

Here is something else to think on. If you won't help plan your life someone else will. Think about it. All you husbands that did not want to plan the wedding, your mother, mother-in-law and wife were more than happy to plan the whole thing. Some of you may have gotten lucky and had food you enjoyed that day and a tux that you really liked or did not mind, but some unlucky gentlemen ended up with a menu he was sure was not from this world and he was forced to wear a pink bow tie that to this day makes him look at his wife funny each time he remembers or catches a glimpse of the wedding pictures. We can joke about this but it is true. The choice not to plan leaves decisions made that are not in favor of the true vision. You want to know why because someone had a vision and someone else did not, when you have no vision you are volunteering to play a role in someone else's plan. I don't know about you but I like to be a part of the decision making not a part of the after affect.

We have choices; we can choose to feel successful and become successful or feel like losers and become losers. Yes, it is that simple. In every business or business plan the company has goals and a mission. That is every successful business or business plan. What makes you think that your life or your business is any different? Think about the last vacation you went on. Did you plan it? How did it go? It probably sucked big time if you did not plan it or let someone else plan the whole thing. Make the choice to plan your life, to organize what it is you want and desire.

So now some of you are excited. Okay that is great, but you just deflated yourself because you started to think about the money. **STOP!** Do you even know how many people have made plans first and find the money later. You cannot let something so small stop your elevation. Yes, I said something so small. Money is the least of your worries at this point. Okay some of you are ready to throw this book at me because you are looking at some serious financial situations, but you can relax. My goal is to get you to see pass the money for a moment. Yes, money is my friend and I treat my friends very, very well, but my friends don't master me I master them.

If you sit and look at the money you don't have, you are also looking at the money you won't have. You are destroying yourself; you are cutting off the future before the vision has even hit the page. Trust me the plan will bring the money. The plan makes the dream real, and then the dream begins to become alive. You have got to plan in order to put things in order, in order to gain a prospective. You know it is the prospective that awards you the goal. Once you understand your vision and expand it on paper you have expanded and created it in your imagination. This is where it takes shape and form, where it gains life. Now that it has that life in you, you are ready to share it with others. You see these goals for you so clearly and you are able to articulate them so well now people are excited to help you and your vision. They want to give any help they can to move you forward.

For example, let's say you want to go to school to get your marketing degree. You have set the goal; write it down, research the schools both off and online that would be best for you and now you need to fund the dream. You are talking to some friends at a dinner party sharing your passion for your new idea and your dream to make it happen. Jackpot, as you are telling your story someone at the table just came into some extra cash and they are so excited about the plans you have made they want to help. Oh yes, this happens, I have been on both ends of this scenario the help and the helper, and each time the vision was there.

Plan, Plan, Plan! What about the staff? *Plan*!

10

What about the office? *Plan*! What about the funding? *Plan*! What about the car note? *Plan*! My girlfriend/boyfriend thinks this is a stupid idea. *Plan*! They are probably just mad they did not think of it first or they are afraid that you will succeed, and in that case, goal number one should be to replace them in the morning. I was taught not to chase, but replace.

If someone does not fit the vision don't stop dreaming. You find out if they have a real place in the dream and if not guess what? Replace them. No love lost, you are just working on your happiness, your time to shine. You know half the people in your life right now may not fit into your plan, but again I ask you, *who's life is this?* Are you living for them or for you? Trust me if someone put a million dollars in their hand and said the only condition to keeping the money was walking away from you, they would run. Don't believe me let's start a game show. We can call it love 'em or leave 'em. This is not to say that you are going to be alone at the top, that saying is such a myth. You are never alone at the top the others are just in the background cheering you on. You will meet with your right connections as your goals and plans begin to take shape. Release the dead weight and move forward with the plan.

The key to claiming your life back and creating order and happiness is planning. Then the next step is to place action to that plan. Step out look into what it takes to make each goal move toward success and completion. Then begin to take those steps one by one. Soon you will turn around and need to create all new steps and plans because you will find all the old ones are complete. So as you remember that this is your life, see the vision, write it down, and listen to your heart. It can all be yours, therefore you should be living your dreams, begin to plan begin to hold the vision.

~See Yourself Whole, See Yourself Rich~

Chapter Two

Something people don't understand is the fact that you have to see yourself where you want to be. You cannot say, "I want to be successful," but look in the mirror each day and see a loser. You have to see and feel the life you desire. Go to the Mercedes lot and feel the car you want, test drive it. Learn what that experience is like so that you begin to see yourself living in that experience. Dress the role you want to play; this gives you a feel for the outcome beforehand.

What does it mean to see yourself whole? You

have to see yourself with all the good the universal is pushing at you. See yourself in the beautiful houses, the new offices, in the great cars, in the wonderful marriage with the beautiful children. If you can see it you can have it, but first you must be able to see it. Something my husband and I did when we first got married was, create a vision board. We took pictures from websites that represented the things we wanted and pasted them together on a single sheet of paper and then taped it next to the bed, that way it was their before we went to bed and there when we woke up. There was no way to not see what we wanted in our lives. Praise God! Each and everything on that vision board has come into our lives over the last seven years in one way or another, and now we have an even bigger vision board with bigger dreams.

I remember when I woke one day and decided the people and things around me were boring and I needed something new and fresh in my life. I decided I was going to school, to college. I had plans to become a fashion designer. It had always been a dream, but now I could see me going to school for it, I was determined to make it happen. I called the school that day and was told only two seats remained and classes started the following week. I had nothing I needed to start school, not even the registration fee, but I did have the vision for what I wanted. I saw myself going to the school and I did. I obtained one of the last two seats and started school the next week. It did not matter what I had in my hands, the vision created what I needed to make it happen.

If you want something bad enough you have to see yourself in it. I am not just saying this, I am living it. I see the success I want, I see it so much that reality has been nonexistent until it turned and shaped itself into the vision, the desire, the goals I have set. I saw myself with the nannies, the butler, the drivers and the mansions. It did not matter that I was sleeping on someone's couch at the time because I was really seeing myself sleeping on a

California king in my mansion.

It does not matter what is looking at you it only matters what you are looking at. Who are you seeing in the mirror? What are you seeing in your driveway? What do you see as success? Can I tell you what you see as success is exactly what you are going to get. Think about it, if you are not able to see yourself successful why should or would anyone else? Ask yourself this, what is success to you? I used to work with children that thought success was making it to jail with their brothers, uncles, and cousins. This is a very sad fact, but success means something different to everyone. Success to me is peace, peace in my home, peace in my mind, peace in my spirit, peace in my finances. As long as my family operates in peace I am successful. I accomplished my goals.

However, in business success takes on another hat for me, in business I need to see growth, expansion, demand for my goods and/or services.

That is a successful business for me, a business that always enlarges the vision and completes the tasks accurately. So what is success to you? Can you see yourself in that success?

One thing I don't allow clients to do with me is complain. You can tell me the problem quickly so that we can address the real underlying issues, but we are not spending an hour rehearsing the soap opera they call their life. That may sound mean, but you have to understand that what you breathe into, you give life to. If I let you complain to me about the hurts how will they go away? When you harp on it you see it, you don't see the change, you don't see the cause, and you don't see the way out. I am in the business of getting you to see the new you, not the you that is terrorizing your life experience.

When a client enters my company we see the potential. Our whole system works from potential, but if the client is not able or willing to see their own potential our service is useless. I have had clients tell me I expect too much, NO YOU DON'T EXPECT ENOUGH! These same clients come back to me later and are so grateful that I pushed them to see the greatness within them, their true potential. However, you may not be so lucky as to have someone like me that will coach you into your potential. That is willing to see you the way you truly are, in that case you "need" to see yourself successful because you are the only one who can.

I mentioned earlier that you should go test drive the car you want. Well do the same with the house; go to open houses in the neighborhood you want to live in. Ride around the neighborhood, shop in the supermarkets in that neighborhood; take your clothes to the cleaners there.

If you are looking for the perfect marriage go dress shopping for the wedding gown, try it on, pick out the head piece and go to some bridal expos. There is no such thing as jinxing yourself. If you think you are jinxing yourself then of course it will never happen. The mind is a powerful thing. What you need to do is see yourself in the role of a wife, in the role of a woman planning the big day. If the business is the goal, start going to seminars, go to other businesses that are in the same field find out what it feels like in that environment.

Feeling and seeing are the keys in this case you have to see your way to the finish line. Don't say what you can't see. That is totally irrelevant and will close the door on whatever it is you are claiming not to see. You won't see it, you know why, because you just said you can't. You have to open your eyes to your true self to your real future. See the you that has it all, the whole you is the true you. The sooner you see yourself rich the sooner it will be. See the money in your bank accounts, see the cars in the driveway, and see the family. See your way to the top!

The more you see the more you will have. This is why dreaming big is so important. You want to dream big in the first place because you don't want to end this life and realize you could have had more if you just would have dreamed a little bigger. I have an argument for those that say "Oh I'll dream this much for now then as that comes I'll dream a little more." You will not dream a little more because you will be so content with the little you bit you received. Nine times out of ten you were not really sure you were going to get anything so now you are ready to settle for what you did get. This is small thinking. It takes a rare person to say, "oh well I received this, let me see if I can get more." Many call those people greedy, but you know what, they managed to ask and because they asked they received, they saw the possibility to have more and they acted. You may not be a repeat asker, so dream as big as you can the first time I see that for yourself.

Even when the dream is large you may receive some of the rewards in parts, but this is fine. This is okay, you move a step at a time but it is important to move toward the vision and have a clear focus of that vision. You will find that as the pieces come together the full puzzle will come into view.

~Delete the Negatives~

Chapter Three

In order to have success you have to, have to, have to delete all negativity. That means your negative thoughts as well as the negative thoughts and actions of those around you. It is hard enough trying to encourage yourself and keeping your own fears and doubts in check. You don't need the fear and doubt chorus to come help you. I always tell my clients to keep things to their self. Many of them don't understand this at first and battle with it because they want to share their success and progress. However, not everyone you think is in your corner truly is. You start telling them about your success and they will come up with all types of craziness to get your mind unfocused.

People will fill your head with whatever they can to stop your progress. "Be careful, money does not grow on trees," sorry but last time I checked yes it does, where does paper come from? "Well you know you need to be good at school to finish," ok that is what studying is for to get better, pass the classes and finish, that has always been the formula for school. Every school that is honorable has tutors, if you need help it is there. "You know I tried to buy a house and that was a mess," and so was their credit, not to mention they owe tons of court fines, this has nothing to do with you. Are you seeing the point? You have to run from these conversations or don't give them a chance to breath in your life. You just don't need it!

I grew up not knowing or understanding no. The word itself infuriates me to no end. *What is that?* For every no there is a very loud, very clear YES!

The word "no" is like a serious challenge to me, it is challenging me to draw out the yes. I remember my second car I was in my early twenties and needed a new car. I went to the used car dealership where I got my first car at 19, they told me no. They could not do the trade in and I should try back in a year or something like that. I was so mad; I just knew that now was the time for me to get a brand new car. A few weeks later I went to a different dealership knowing this time I was getting a car and oh yes, I did leave that lot with a brand new car that had 3 miles on it and I was paying the note I wanted to pay.

Strip no from your vocabulary unless using it for declining bad business ventures or useless relationships, no is not an option when it comes to your success. If you want a house so what the first 20 banks said "no", bank number 21 has that yes! You just need to look at the situation and see why the no is there, is the house you are looking at too small and you are not dreaming big enough? Are you trying to move someone that is not supposed to live with you into the house? Is it not the right neighborhood for you? It could be that the no is coming for you to make one adjustment to your plans.

You cannot play yourself short you have to get focused on your goals and see nothing but good in them. Count it all joy, even the hard times or hard roads have great lessons and opportunities. You take the *nos* and make them experiences for your advancement. Learn something from difficulties don't just give up. What I learned from the no with the car was that I needed a new car, not a used one. Used is not what the universe wanted for me. I deserved better.

That is something you must get in the habit of knowing. Say it with me, "*I deserve better!*" When you start thinking to yourself, "well maybe this is too much to handle" or "I think I'm dreaming too big," stop and tell yourself, "I deserve better!" Look yourself in the mirror each morning and each evening before you go to sleep and say, "I deserve better!" Say it so much that when negative experiences try to make their way in your life you spring into your stance and shout, "*I deserve better!*" Oh yes, this means you, "*You deserve better!*" I take these words very seriously. These words pushed me into a new season, a new experience. I decided what I was looking at was not my truth, "*I deserved better!*" Sure enough better came knocking at my door with a bow on it.

You have to distance yourself from negative thoughts, ideas and people. All of these just make success more difficult to come by. Embrace positive thoughts, positive ideas, and positive people. If you know someone is never happy to hear about your good fortune don't invite them into your experience. Their energy alone makes the milk and honey sour. I have been around people that I know are not supporters of my vision and they have let me know so by the energy they give off. I tell you, they are smiling the whole time but the body language is so negative, in such an off the chart manner, that I make myself ghost to them. I do not do the drama. Please don't try to bring it to me.

Some people will have a very hard time with this part because they love the drama. They do a song and dance for it. Leave the drama on Broadway this is your life, your business, the drama does not belong. That means do not take the phone calls from the friends and family that bring the mess with them. "Hey cousin how are you, I hope you are doing great!" You respond, "Yes I am!" And here they go, "well you know things are not that great over here the kids are sick, grandma is in the hospital, and the oldest boy is in jail." You did not even see this coming and did not have the time to stop it. The better thing to do would be to ignore the call in the first place you know they never have anything good to talk about anyway.

Now some of you have business partners that

display this behavior, the negative, this will never work, but in case you get it to I am going to ride the wave partner. **86 them**! They are the main reason the business is failing. They don't believe in the vision. Some of you have partners that are there to make sure you don't succeed. Be mindful who you let in your gates. You must protect your mind gate, your ear gate and your eye gates. Don't allow people to place the fear, stress and doubt in your mind. Approach your goals with an open mind and positive thoughts. See success in every action. Know you are a great success story. Quiet the chaos by ignoring the negativity. You don't have to be rude just remove yourself from the drama, the universe will make sure they get the point and disappear.

You will begin to find that as you see results you will not be able to entertain foolishness. You will be too busy enjoying your happiness and moving towards your goals. You will no longer let these things limit you and your potential. I was recently told by my mentor that those that are not part of the vision will not even be able to enter into the experience. Once you begin to strengthen the vision and move into it those negative things and people will find that access has been denied. Only positive people, positive things will find their way next to you. It is your job to trust and believe in you. Anyone doing otherwise just press delete, don't negotiate, don't fight, just delete.

~Handling and Circulating Your Money~

Chapter Four

The biggest key to success is balance. Many fail at success because of lack of balance in business and in financing. You must create the harmony in your wallet. Come on a journey with me so I can tell you how to create this harmony. Relax open your mind and envision yourself fully understanding the harmony in your wallet. The way to create this harmony is to stop being cheap. Truly wealthy people do not hold a tight fist. They are givers, they share their wealth. Money is not meant to be horded it is meant to be circulated. That is why they call it cash flow. Something that is stored up is not being circulated it is just sitting in one place collecting unwanted dust. At the same time you are not to over circulate in any direction. The universe is created through and from order and balance. Everything has its place, time and purpose.

In church it is called seedtime and harvest, in the world it is reaping what you sow. What is to be understood is that you cannot plant all apples and expect to have apples and oranges equally. In order to harvest both equally you would need to have both seeds in equal portions. I am a giver I love to give, but I spent a lot of my life giving more than I received. I made sure everyone was taken care of before me. This turned out to be a big lesson for me, because I learned there has to be balance. You cannot go through life never giving or giving just enough nor can you go through life giving everything and forget to partake in your blessings, your harvest. You must be willing to give all if necessary, but also willing to take the necessary actions to see fruitfulness and success in your experience.

Does that make sense to you yet? What you need to see is that you give to receive, although you are giving with the right intentions, with the heart of a giver. You live to give. You never stop giving. However, there are times and seasons where you give out and times and seasons where you give accordingly and plant into your increase as well, in order to continue to give. All of my clients learn, from the start, the law of 10 percent. Your success, your lawful success depends on it. What do I mean by lawful? The universe must obey law, and seed time or sowing or tithing or whatever you call it, it is a Universal law. You must honor the 10 percent, not just 10 percent of what you feel is covenant but 10 percent of all.

Now before I lose you because this is where people begin to sweat. Understand the seed only leaves your hand, never your life. It will come back to you in one measure or another, but always in the manner in which it is given. Pay very close attention to this part, because I learned this the super duper hard way, you absolutely reap what you sow. If you give to the sick it will return to you in the form of sickness. If you give to the poor it will return to you in some form of poverty. If you give to the rich guess what you will receive the return in a rich state. This may sound harsh but it is true. Think about it, you give your money to a school with a bad reputation, when you graduated that bad reputation tried to follow you. You are getting what you paid for.

Here is another example you volunteer to work in a country stricken with poverty. Which there is nothing wrong with this, this is someone's calling. However, each year, each day, each minute given to volunteering is a year, day, or minute that individual is not creating an increase for their own life. They have volunteered to become stricken with poverty. Now everyone can act like they are self-righteous and would rather give service then make money, but money makes life and change happen. Even volunteers have to ask for money to continue volunteering.

This all boils down to, what results do you want to see in your life? If you want to see wealth then sow your 10 percent into a wealthy outlet. If you want to see what being sick is like sow your 10 percent into sickness. This same concept is why balance is important, because a volunteer who understands balance would take the time to invest in his or hers own growth. A wealthy person understands balance, they will give to wealthy charities as well as donate to a children's hospital but in a balanced form that does not create the undesired outcomes.

I guess what should be said here is that you are buying into a consciousness when you give into something. You want to be mindful of the consciousness you become aware of. Let's face it when you give into something you research the area to make sure it is good ground to sow into. At least I hope you do, if not I need to put a bonus chapter in for you. At that time you are opening yourself to that area. This is when you have to make sure you are stepping out of the experience, if it is a consciousness you do not desire to walk away with. So it is possible to give to the sick without taking on the sick state of mind you just have to be aware to create the healthy mind state around you and those involved in your actions.

Now for those having a hard time dealing with the 10 percent, get over it because that is just the beginning. That is just what allows you to follow law. You make your way to wealth by what you give over the ten percent. This is where your discipline is learned. This is where you learn to give all when necessary and create in all giving. See we create through our seeds. You must always have seed in the ground but discipline teaches you what ground and when. There is a time when you empty out to create room for increase and then there is a time to take that increase to grow it to empty out again for a bigger increase. I found that when you give somehow the giving always makes sure you have more to give. I can feel when it is time to give all for a breakthrough.

I will give an example, I lived an abundant life in 2007, but it was time for me to increase again to an even greater level. I emptied out all I had to my church ministry because I understand the Universal law of seedtime and harvest. I needed to create the void in my life, in the universe, that would allow me to come into a greater harvest. I understood what would happen to my financial situation, but it was not ideal at the time anyway because I saw myself with more. Understand abundance can have its limits in consciousness; my consciousness outgrew that level of abundance.

So my husband and I did what was necessary we took our faith and what we knew about God and his universal laws and we gave out. Oh yes we ended up with a bunch of mess looking back at us but our faith and wisdom pushed us forward to the harvest time. Anytime you challenge the limits of harvest you are opposed, this is the test of your faith in what you are doing. It is a process and in the end you see the process was necessary to bring change.

Now we dwell in a tremendous increase and when the increase came we understood it was time to now take the blessings and increase them in order to create more seed and opportunity. The universe, God, does not want you to live out of balance or in that over righteous state where now you are giving him back the blessing. You are to give according to the ten percent law and then create harmony with your increase. It is really a harmony you create with your thoughts, because it is your thinking that allows you to create the size of the harvest. Your thoughts, values and predetermined limitations are what help to create the proper balance in your life.

Please don't misunderstand this; you do not stop giving by any means. You are just taking your talents and increasing them for your purpose. You master money, do not let it master you. Being able to empty out in the first place shows you are not a slave to money. It shows you are willing to release in order to increase, it shows you know how to grow and create balance. You are mastering the art of circulation.

Now let's talk about money. Money is your friend, if you cannot believe or accept that than you will not find wealth. Money is not a dirty word or concept. It is what people do with and for it that can become truly dirty. Money is just the material substance that helps produce manifestation. However, money has ears in its spiritual or universal form. This is why you must be mindful of what you say you do and don't have or what you can't and won't have.

Say with me **"money is my friend."** My mentor

taught me how to treat my money, how to wine and dine her, how to call her in. I learned to play with my money and make her feel wanted in my family. Money knows it always has a friend in me. I trust in God, but money trusts in me. Do you see the difference? By trusting the universe, the Supreme Being, God, you create balance in your supply. Money is neither your center focus nor your master, which allows you to then focus on the important factors.

Factor #1: I do it because I love it.

Answer this question; do you know why it is you do what you do? If you say it is the money you are in it for the wrong reasons. Your why is not strong enough to get you the results you seek. How many people wake up in the morning and are truly happy with what they do for a living? "Do for a living," this puts a distaste in my mouth, because most people are not working for a living, they are living to work. Most people are working on a JOB or as I love to hear is called, a "Just Over Broke," that are literally killing them. I can remember when I worked on one particular job and I would hope to get in a car accident or something just so I didn't have to go. I would wake up in the morning sick to my stomach and after a holiday or the last day of the weekend I would have the worst attitude, which by the way I did not realize until my husband made the connection at a party we attended the night before a vacation was coming to an end.

I finally realized I had lost the love I had for my job, if I ever had any. I hated it! I was there for the pay check, something I never do. I walk away from a job that makes me unhappy in a heartbeat, but here I was working for money! I quickly found a solution to that, I left and remembered to do what I loved first and make money second. I recreated the balance in my life.

As long as you chase money you will do things you don't want to do. As I said earlier you don't chase you replace. You create freedom from the panting. Relax and you will start to see the opportunities not the facts that try to block you. Money arrives when it sees a comfortable environment. If things feel uncomfortable money will circle the situation till you relax.

Factor # 2: The plan

Money also likes organization and order. This is why planning has been stressed so much. Money wants to know there is a plan for it; that you are not going to just have it sitting there doing nothing. Also keep in mind that what you plan for you receive. If you plan for a rainy day you are going to have a rainy day. You planned for it, sent out some seriously nice invitation for it. You created that very thing. So plan for things you can enjoy and money will, willingly join the party to help you enjoy the plans.

Factor #3: Keep the circulation

Money is to be circulated I cannot stress this more. You should never spend money, to spend money is to end it, and to circulate is to send it out to comeback. Learn how to hula hoop! Get in the middle of your finances and send them spinning around you. Send in your tithes, pay your bills with enjoyment, go shopping, start the second business. Send in your tithes, buy a new house, give to a book foundation, go shopping to furnish the new house, start the third business. Are you getting the hang of this, circulate.

Factor #4: Diversity

You have to diversify your investments, in order to see your money grow. Don't be afraid to watch your money grow in different pots, it helps the soil breath, and your roots have room to expand. I am sure you have heard don't put your eggs all in one basket. Study, research and learn your best avenues to expand your money.

This leads me to the four streams of income.

Successful individuals have at a minimum four streams of income. Think about basketball players or any athlete. They have income from the team salary, they have endorsements, and some will commentate on a sports show as well as making guest appearances. That adds up a four, now many of the players that carry wisdom also have businesses and real estate. They understand that to maintain their luxurious lifestyle they need multiple streams of income.

My clients know that I take the four streams to the max. I show them how to create finances that supports and circulates continually throughout their streams. This way they never experience lack ever again once operating in the flow I help them structure. If one stream dries up the others are the life support in which the stream is recreated or redeveloped. Notice streams circulate, just as your money should.

Now that we have an order set up with giving

and an understanding of circulation it is time to look at handling your money business. I have been taught by wise counsel that it is critical to take care of tithes, offerings and taxes first. This keeps you in right standing with all law, universal and governmental. I do not buy a stick of gum before taking care of the tithes, offering and taxes. This way you are sure you have taken care of all your needs as far as obligations are concerned and now you can focus on you and the running of your company.

So let's recap. Money is our friend, not our master. Money must always be in circulation. The key to maintaining wealth is balance and you need at least four streams of income to maintain a healthy financial balance. Now you are ready to play.

~*Your Own Boss*~

Chapter Five

Being your own boss is the greatest thing in the world. However, it is a great responsibility, this is one of the reasons many people will never run their own business. They are not ready for the responsibility; it is a heavy concept but a rewarding one. We create our surroundings, understanding and admitting that is the first step to taking responsibility. Why not be your own boss and be accountable for the living you create. Being responsible is not as scary as it sounds; it just requires focus, determination and passion for what you do, as well as organization.

You create the hours you desire and the levels of practice you wish to move in. If you want to start a company that is in the business of operating locally that is your decision. Most people are overwhelmed by the idea of a business, but you should relax. Find yourself in the thought pattern that allows you to see success as a business owner, feel the accomplishment, the determination, as you hear the confidence and pride in your voice as you tell people what you do for a living. I find that every time I complete a business I am so relieved and I am left wondering why I thought it would be so much harder to do. It never is. Things are always easier than they look.

You must be willing to put the time and effort into your own career. Being afraid to ask questions or fill out the necessary paperwork is only a lie you tell yourself. Fear is the road block that needs to be destroyed in order to move forward and grow. The initial steps to becoming an entrepreneur are minimal compared to the great outcome of success and stability.

"What are the benefits," you ask. For starters you are not limited to the level of success you can achieve in your future. You are not stuck in a job where you are waiting years for a promotion that may never happen. Being your own boss is just that you decide how big the company will be and how far you will go. If you feel something can be done better guess what you can change it and do it better. You don't have to go to your supervisor and make a suggestion or sit around complaining about what the company is doing wrong. In addition to calling the shots you are creating your own happiness. You are running the business you desire. You are not sitting at someone else's job looking angry and bitter. You are taking control.

What a lot of people fail to think about is the future of their family. When you become your own boss you are creating an opportunity for the family. You are earning the income for the better living, the better education and the better opportunities. Your children are seeing through you what entrepreneurship truly is. In addition, your business is something they can grow into and run someday. You are modeling a successful life for your family. You are teaching your family discipline in order to grow your business.

You will also find that once you start the first business it becomes habit and you begin to feel the need to start the next venture. One business is not enough; you begin to see your true potential for more. Being a business owner gives you a sense of accomplishment and a drive to move forward and expand. However, not everyone expands into multiple businesses some just know how to continuously grow and expand on the one big idea, making it an ever evolving entity.

One thing I had to learn is that others can always see your ability for leadership. This is why they love having you around as an employee, but are not so keen on your ideas to be an entrepreneur. They want you working for them, leading their business to success. You are valuable to their company. Well guest what you are just as valuable to your own, maybe even more so because it is your baby, your creation. A true leader will teach you all they know to send you off on your way when you are ready. While building my companies I would meet people that would totally ignore my dreams and try to use my talents for their business and needs. This was a problem for me initially because I did not know how to say no or strike a balance. I should have worked to help them while I helped myself. Not! I would let them bleed me of knowledge and strength and be too tired and unfocused for my plans.

Many of you I am sure are the same way. I say to you release. Release the people that call you up with the next best business idea they just know you are perfect to help them with. You have to put you in order first. Giving there may be someone that can give the boost you need by working for them, but I guarantee you they will be the one that will function with or without you, not the one that needs you to build. Be the captain of your own ship and then maybe you can share the wisdom of leadership with others. However, don't get caught in a business or job that is not yours where you become the boss and are not receiving the benefits.

Labor with love on your ideas, increase your mental giants. We all have them, ideas that are so large, so intense that you have to put them to paper and bring them to life. These ideas are the gateway to being your own boss.

Please remember nobody represents you like you. You become the boss to engineer the legacy you want to leave in this lifetime. I once heard a very well-known gentleman speak about the dash in the middle. You are born on one date and die on another, but the most important part of life is the dash in the middle. How are you being represented by your dash?

You were born with creative money making ideas for a reason. You are meant to create, you were meant to succeed. You are meant to create, you are meant to succeed. You are meant to live a life of comfort, but it is all in your hands. Becoming your own boss opens this potential to meet your business mastery. There are so many things in life we live to master. Being able to meet mastery goals satisfies your soul and mind. So why not please yourself by taking a step. Set your mind on it, grow yourself into the idea. BE YOUR OWN BOSS.

~Why Four Streams~

Chapter Six

Earlier on you heard me speak of four streams of income. I would like to touch on the concept a little more here. I learned this from my mentor and then put it on steroids. If you ever read the bible in the book of Genesis it speaks of the main river that broke into four streams that flowed out of the Garden of Eden. *[10]And a river went out of Eden to water the garden; and from thence it was parted, and became into four heads. [11]The name of the first is Pison: that is it which compasseth the whole land of Havilah, where there is gold; [12]And the gold of that land is good: there is bdellium and the onyx stone.* [13]*And the name of the second river is Gihon: the same is it that compasseth the whole land of Ethiopia.* [14]*And the name of the third river is Hiddekel: that is it which goeth toward the east of Assyria. And the fourth river is Euphrates* (Genesis 2: 10-14). These four streams kept the flow, watered and nourished. Don't you want to live a life that is watered and nourished?

Your finances should support and work each other. If you have a well-balanced cash flow you have no concern for lack. Balance! Balance usually comes in fours, north, south, east and west; summer, winter, spring and fall. A table or chairs for that matter has four legs.

The number four is a number of increase. Think about it 2 plus 2 equals four. 2 times 2 equals four. You always want to add or multiple in your life. The number four represents foundation. Having four streams of income creates a strong foundation. Your foundation is what keeps you standing.

When I was completing my MBA I took a class on strategic planning. In the class we learned about the BCG Matrix (the Boston Consulting Group Matrix). This matrix gives a business view of the importance of four streams of income. Corporate industries use this matrix to analyze the strengths and weaknesses in their company. It allows them to see which divisions are in a questionable state and are not generating as much cash as they need to function. Which divisions are stars bringing in the money and having great potential for growth and profits. Which divisions are the cash cows providing excesses of profits allowing a firm to milk them. As well as the fourth section that are dogs showing no growth. The matrix shows the cash flow.

This is what you want your finances to do, show you the cash flow. Where is your money? If you look at the four quadrants in the matrix you see the circulation process that will keep your finances flowing.

Let me explain a little more. Joe has a coffee shop. He sells coffee and sandwiches. Joe does well in his first year selling enough to cover the bills and to restock supplies. However, Joe is not seeing a return that is pleasing to his wife's spending habits. Joe comes to my office and I explain to him that things are not overflowing because of one simple factor. He only has one stream of income coming into his home and into his business. He can change his financial situation very easy by adding a new source of income.

I tell Joe to start with the business. He can add revenue by selling mugs and other items behind the register. Now his business is up two streams. Next I advise him to add Internet service customers can pay to use. Now he has three streams of income. Now to be creative, Joe's wife likes to make baskets, so I advise him to start a website to serve Internet customers that buy his ground coffee. His wife can make baskets with coffee and mugs and they can ship them as well as sell the baskets in the store.

Stream number four.

We understand that at any time one of the four streams Joe is now offering can lack steady income flow, but with the generation of the other three it gives Joe room to breathe and to think about what is going on around him. If the Internet services fall in profits in April Joe does not need to sweat. He has just become aware that changes need to happen. Increase in marketing the Internet service, a web party, perhaps new computers or maybe it is time to remove the Internet and bring in live entertainment.

Do you see the benefits of the four streams? When they are working together, even if not all at the same level you face security and overflow, but in a season when one stream runs dry you always have three others that sustain you until you revise or replace the weakest link. With four streams of income you can afford to lose a stream or two and still not face panic. If Joe wants to take security to the next level he will begin to create streams of income outside of the coffee shop as well, anything that he is passionate about that generates income.

One of the main reasons people freak out when they lose their job is because they only had one stream of income. Their job served as their end all and be all. They never thought to start an Internet business or open the bike shop they always dreamed of having on the side or they never got around to writing that book that has been dancing in their head for the last five years.

It is much easier than you think to produce four streams of income. Having a rental property or two is a good start. If you invest wisely, picking up a piece of property in a great area, which you managed to get for a great price, you are in the money. Your maintenance fees are so minimal you are walking away with a monthly steal. And this is possible because you planned ahead. You studied the real estate to see that this would truly be another stream of income for you.

Are you seeing the importance of planning, circulating and multiple steams of income? This should make sense even to the guy who is not ready to leave his job, but wants to start a business anyhow. One income sustains the other, which in turn sustains you. You have the means to expand and grow.

This system also creates checks and balances in your finances. When you see a stream that is drying up you begin to question the waters before it is too late. Can your other streams save the one or will the one diminish the others? Never become complacent with your cash flow. When you do, you become the boiling frog. You are sitting in the pot not noticing that the water is getting hotter and hotter until it is too late and you are cooked.

Let your four streams become your eyes and ears, your indicators. Keep an eye on the changes to your wealth so that you know how to change. Let the cushion of the four streams help you remain in the driver's seat but notice when the cushion is telling you it needs to be reupholstered.

Why four streams? So your well doesn't run dry. Four streams of income is just another form of planning your goals and your way to success. Take time to evaluate your streams of income. How many streams are flowing into your home? Is there at least one stream from everyone in the home? How can you increase those streams? How many of those streams are coming from your passion? If you are ready to finally build wealth and success, be honest with yourself about these questions. Don't get caught without a stream.

~Money "Matters"~

Chapter Seven

I thought it would be a great idea to show you the truth and purpose of money. So first let's throw away all the garbage about money being evil. The last time I went to the store to get food I needed money. To top that, I don't remember the twenty dollar bill bursting into flames or giving me a sinister laugh when it came out of my pocketbook. Money is what we use to get things. Money is a friend, but are you being a friend to money.

Stop saying what you don't need! If you did not need money you would not be reading this book.

No one is impressed by poverty so stop trying to be modest about your desires. Yes, you would like to have a nice new expensive car. Yes, you do want a nice new house. Yes, you do want a vacation. Yes, you would like to pay all your bills on time and still have money for food and a shopping spree at the mall. But if you continue to lie to yourself and the universe that all you need is this or all you need is that, guess what this and that is all you are going to get.

The key to all of this, to everything in life is knowing that you can have nothing you are not aware of having. Neither can you have anything you feel you don't desire or feel you don't deserve. Money is a substance of the universe. It follows your vibration. If you are vibrating at a level that says you don't desire her, money will not date you. It is as simple as that.

So stop focusing on where the money is coming from for a minute and just focus on the fact that it is here. Money is your friend, it has missed you dearly and wants to treat you to some new things, take you to some new places. Introduce you to her other friends and family. Think about it money can do all of this for you. All money wants you to do is realize that money matters. Money is not filthy, it is not evil; it is a friend indeed. I don't know about you but I could use a few friends that want to take me out shopping.

Money only requires that you respect it. Not worship, respect. We give respect where respect is due. How do you know the difference? When you can walk away from something you have mastered it. You are at a point where you are not worshipping a thing. It is not the master of you. When you can walk away from a million dollar deal because you know it is wrong and the deal will harm more than it will help you are mastering money. You are placing money where you should, because anything, or anyone that loves you can leave your life but it will always return. That million dollars will know you had respect for it and others around you, it will seek you out and make its way into your life in a good and appreciate manner because you did not bad mouth the money you turned down the deal. You placed the value in the right order.

Stop bad mouthing money. I mean this. It is insane to look at money as the cause of a problem. This takes us back to accountability. The two million dollar car did not run the light and cause the accident, the driver did. The twelve million dollar salary did not make the CEO harass the secretary. He decided to do that on his own. Nine times out of ten if he was a manager at Wendy's he would have sexually harassed a worker there as well. If you are looking at a situation that seems like money caused it look a little deeper. I bet your fingerprints are all over the problem. You created that mess somehow, and now my friend money is taking the blame. Well I have news for you, money does not like being blamed for things it did not do and as long as you blame her, she is not going to come around.

Money is waiting on you right now to change your mind and your vocabulary toward her. Notice I keep saying her. Money is a sophisticated lady. That is why she waits for you to first respect her, then plan a purpose for her before she shows up to hang around you and date you. Money wants to be taken out, shown the finer things in life. Money only takes on it masculine form during seedtime. This is when money looks to show its pride. Money is proud of you when you operate as a sower. You are allowing money to plant its seeds to implant itself in your life. Money wants to birth dreams. When it is in its feminine state it produces the desires of your heart. When it is in its masculine form it impregnates your future your harvest. Once again in the form of a never ending cycle, money is meant to circulate.

That was a lot to digest right there so I'll say it another way. You sow to grow and as you grow money returns to you to show you all life has to offer. The more you sow the more you grow. The more you grow the more that money shows you. Get it?

Prepare a place for your money mentally and physically. Open your mind and plan the idea that will draw her in. Map it out make it look good. Go get a new wallet or purse. Open a new account. Money loves that, when you are so ready to entertain her that you set up a brand new account just for her arrival. Now know you deserve all the new money due to you, watch your mouth. Don't limit the amount of friends your money plans to bring along. Your money may be coming as a party of millions you don't want to talk her friends out of continuing the journey. Some people talk what should be millions into thousands. Words are powerful, be mindful of them. Remember money has ears.

~*Taste the Success*~

Chapter Eight

Now that we have placed the mind in order and have the focus necessary to plan and attract the money for the plan, it is time to hit the ground running. We are at the point where the plan is finished and you are ready to put yourself out there.

Whatever the goal maybe, the key to getting to the finish line is to start. I studied project management during my MBA studies. I have a Master's in Business, in marketing and project management. One of the tasks in strategic planning and project management is to plan implementation.

See it is understood that people plan and plan and plan and guess what they never move behind that plan. Well this is not going to be you. You have put your heart into this plan and you owe it to yourself to step out on your plan.

You have to make a move. If you set the goal to go to college, you have apply to the schools, you have to research which schools are best for you and your major. Though I would love to help I can't do it for you nor can anyone else. You have to say this is it, "I am taking control."

Maybe your goal is to start an Internet business. By now you should have the vision on paper and now is the time to tighten that vision up by moving on the site, put together your marketing tools and begin telling people about your site. It is on you to start things up.

With every step you take, you are getting to taste a piece of your success. You are getting to a place of accomplishment. This is when determination kicks

in because you are seeing the dream take shape.
Every tiny piece of the picture creates the whole.
You will find your frame full in no time; if you stick
to the principles you have been given you will soar.
Success is sweet and the sweetness is reached by
following the formula.

Formula to Success:

1. Sow the seed.

   - Start with your ten percent.

   - Now Stretch. Push beyond your comfort
     zone.

   - Empty out into good ground.

2. Plan.

   - Set your goals.

   - Write a plan.

   - Research.

3. See yourself where you want to be.

   - Let no one stop you.

   - Trim the fat, get rid of distractions.

4. Become friends with money.

- See money in the right way.
5. Make a step.

Set yourself up for the win. If you followed the steps without skipping one you are sure to make the mark. The fact that you have operated in the laws of the universe and begin the process with sowing your seed will bring you increase all by itself. Couple that with seeing yourself in your goals and making the plan plain you are really cooking now.

However, it is important to follow each step and to keep moving forward. Never sit after a win the next one is right around the corner. I see every battle won as a learning experience for the next. That makes me eager to get to the next lesson. Don't be afraid to move on to the next task.

I used to wait for the other shoe to drop, but I learned that when I am too busy engaged in the next step I have no time to look back or wait for the aftershock. This made me see that the only reason the aftershocks used to happen was because I looked back for them. This is why I advise you to move forward right away. Take the next step before you foil the steps you have already taken. Success is yours to have as you continue to move forward.

Once again don't limit yourself. You can have all you can handle in this life. Just see and believe. Once you have decided what success is to you see yourself in it. I was once told by someone who loves me very much to dream big as big as I could and I started to see things I was not aware of before I was able to pull the limits off and see great things for myself. You have to see your supply, taste it and it will meet your demand.

If you are a writer don't just see the finished book. See the number one New York best seller. See the millions of copies sold. See the book tour. Taste the success of a successful writer. So what this is all in your imagination that is where the dream started and that is where it will birth from.

I imagined a husband who loves me and

supports all my dreams and talents when I was younger and that is exactly what I got. And you better believe I wrote down the plan and goal to marry such a husband. The laws don't lie.

I have dreams bigger than life and I am confident that I am going to carry each one out. For one I have sown for them. Next I believe and see me doing them and I continue to plan my way to each dream. I am no different from you. You can do all that I can if you follow the map I have given.

Once you get your first taste you will know it is too good to go back. Let success be your motivator. Let your first taste take you to the next level.

~Mediation – Relaxation~

Chapter Nine

I would be doing you a great disservice if I fail to touch on mediation and relaxation. You need the two to bring harmony to self. You must find the time to reset yourself daily. One reason some people are happy today and a mess tomorrow is because they fail to reset their thoughts and their focus.

Mediation is not as scary as some try to make it seem. We are mediating on something all the time. What you need to understand is that you must become aware of this fact so that you are not mediating on the wrong things. Basically mediation is continued thought in a general direction. So what are you mediating on? I bet I could tell you by looking at your life. Can I tell you that worry is a form of mediation?

So what are you worrying about? Is it the bills, not finding a mate, or maybe failing a class? What you mediate on will become your reality. Now do you see why mediation is important? You must become aware of mediation in order to prevent mediating on the wrong things. Don't say you don't have time to mediate because you are doing it already all day long.

Mediation is another key to getting the desires of your heart. Placing a conscious effort into the process will eliminate those things you don't want. Don't think you need to get all fancy with it, standing on your head, chanting and all that. Sure there are different levels of mediation. Some more intense than others but you can start at your own level. The universe will always meet you at your level.

You will find that the more you become comfortable with the mediation process the more you will find your way into a deep level, a deep peace. My mentor always suggests keeping a pen and paper when meditating. I see it this way, mediation is a place for answers. You go in with questions and come out with answers.

If you are looking for the next step in your business, sit quietly and ask in your mind "what is my next step?" The answer will come to you with time. Sometimes it will be a quick response other times you will have to put in some time. I found it good to write your questions down before you go into mediation, but that's me. I do this because sometimes I go in for one thing and I come out with so much more. I get answers to things and get excited and forget all about my original entry assignment.

Mediation is something that should be enjoyed.

The universe is always talking to us; we just need to slow down long enough to listen. We all enter meditation differently. You need to find the way into your private zone. The way you tap into the vibration of your beginning. I like music and sitting in tight spaces. That has always been my thing.

You will find the best way for you to make your mediation work for you. In the bath tub, candles, maybe in the car in morning as you go to work or after work before you go in the house. The point is to find your zone and get there regularly. This is a great way to restart your day if it starts off as something you are not willing to experience.

There are some great books on mediation that will take you into deeper understanding and give you techniques on how to enter in and out. This is another step you really need to honor. It will help you remain focused on the journey and the destination of your success and help to sustain you once you arrive at your goals. I have written a work called *Don't Forget the Source*. It is a reminder that we sometimes make it to our goals and forget how we get there. Mediation will keep you grounded and connected to your foundation.

It is important to remember the principles that carry you to your success. Going through all the work only to lose yourself is a waste. Meditation is your link to the truth, your door to the true you. It will also lead you to the truth of you. Meditation and meditation in the right direction brings connection and alignment, it brings order.

Now that you understand the reason for meditation we can move to relaxation. Relaxation can come as a result of meditation or as a gateway into meditation, but my intention is to get you to understand its importance. You have to learn to relax. You should never be anxious about anything; it is your right to relax. If you have sown into your harvest, planned your vision, written your goals and made all the moves you can, your next move is to relax.

Patience is key and learning to relax will strengthen your patience. You may say that this is easier said than done, but I want you to know I am not telling you anything I haven't done or experienced. There are times when I have had ridiculous circumstances facing me and I had to find it in myself to relax. I knew my tithes and offerings were in place and I did not plan for the chaos nor did I mediate on it. So my truth was in the relaxation necessary to see pass what was facing me.

When you learn to relax you learn to focus. You are able to keep a clear head and remain focused on the task you are after. Relaxation has a powerful attribute to it. I used to work with children that were emotionally disturbed. They feed off of your energy. Other staff members would want to know what my secret was and that is clear, I know how to relax. The moment you show them anything else they would lose control of themselves and it was downhill from there. Learn to relax.

If your boss is having a bad day and wants to take it out on you, relax. That is his or her problem no need in you partaking in that energy. The kids are having a melt down over ice cream. Relax you being so calm will calm them down. They will see the tantrum is useless and they will move on eventually. Car breaks down on the side of the road, relax. Something is calling your attention relaxing will tell you what and you will be able to address it. Maybe it is something minor and you just need the minor fix to remind you that it is time for your inspection. Or maybe the universe is pushing you to your new car that you have been thinking (mediating) about. Just relax.

You will find that half the things you freak out about are not that serious. If you just relax you will see your way through to a peaceful situation. A lot of people that used to be around me could not understand how I could ignore things that seemed to them and most the rest of the world to be something so major. What good is it going to do if I worry? The more I relax the clearer the solution becomes.

So I challenge you to find peace in all things. Find yourself in meditation and learn to relax. No worries, it is just not that serious really.

~Mentors and Mentorship~

Chapter Ten

I know I have mentioned my mentor a few times.
He always says you should not move through life
without a guide. I firmly believe in this truth. When
you were in middle school you had a teacher. Your
teacher went to school to learn to teach and became
certified to teach you. They had to have experience
to teach you. The school was not going to let the
girl sitting next to you get up and take over the class
for the year. This is the concept you should keep
throughout life, you need someone that has been
where you are trying to go.

Personally, I set a goal I want to find the person who has accomplished that goal on a mastery level and get them to guide me through the process into success. I don't want the advice of someone that is moving in the same lane as me. I need someone with experience, someone that has seen the finish line and knows how I can get to the finish line as well. This individual will not only know how to get through but they will know to tell me which direction will be trouble and which steps I can avoid to stay out of trouble. It won't be a case of the blind leading the blind if you find a mentor that will lead you from experience.

There is nothing wrong with a guide, nothing wrong with saying, "I don't know it all, but I want to learn." Most people want to walk it alone thinking they know it all or know better than everyone else. Even kings have advisors. Having a guide gets you to your goals faster. You are not going to hold yourself accountable the way a great mentor will. My clients know that some days I am the last person they want to see or talk to but when I am done they are going to love me and the hell I put them through because I see the place they want to go and I know how to get them there. It's my job to push them the extra mile to make sure they meet their goals.

It is important to have a mentor and to make sure they are the right mentor for you. One thing I find that people make a mistake with, they will find people make a mistake with a great mentor and make the mistake of stepping out from under them to soon. A great mentor will be in your life for some time. You will find that they are your source of confirmation and that the relationship between you and your mentor is one that should remain a relationship of respect.

I've had people come to me and after a few sessions they decide they can do what I do and they decide to run off to copy the little I have given them. This is all wrong. It's not that I don't want them copying me, a good student should be able to copy, but you must first get all of the lessons. Otherwise, you are now trying to lead others but you have no idea where to or how. You become a talking head, a parrot. You are making mistakes not only with your life now but with others. Sure you may have read this book, listened to me speak a few times even read some of my other works but you have not sat long enough to receive the fullness of the wisdom I have to give you.

I continue to learn from my mentors and intend to continue to learn from the wisdom they carry. When it is time for me to learn from someone else they will give me the wisdom they can but my connection to the mentors I have now will not be break and certainly not prematurely. People would know I have lost my guide and they will know who my guide was as well because I would carry the piece of the true released to me. So I could not even successfully pass the wisdom for my own it would be out of season and sound wrong, confused.

I find it funny when people want to drop their mentors name, but when they spoke you can tell they are either not a good student or they are a student that has walked away too soon. In order to avoid this you need to not only find a mentor but stick to them and pay attention. I once got caught not paying attention and I was corrected on it, but it was a correction that not only set me straight but put me in a focused zone. Never be too proud to take correction from your mentor. They are not trying to embarrass you they are pushing you into your next level. A mentor is a wonderful authority to have in your life. Understanding and respecting authority can be a whole other book on its own. This truth unlocks doors on multiple levels. You cannot reach your full potential with a lack of respect for authority; you are lacking the position of your map without it.

A mentor shows up in the right season to teach you. You as the student must become willing to learn. A mentor can only give you as much as you are willing to receive. When you come before a mentor you drop all titles to learn, if not your ego will hinder your learning process. The reason that two people can have the same mentors and one becomes more successful than the other has nothing to do with one not being as smart as the other, it has all to do with what one was willing to receive and the other one wasn't. Learn to open yourself to receive the lessons given to you. Listen more than you speak. I have a hard time with this even now because I get so excited about learning but I am learning to listen and take notes so that my questions and discussion can come at a later date and time.

You should also make it a point to seek not only all the writings of your mentor, which will show you their evaluation, but find out what they are reading and have read. This will give you insight to so much and will help you understand where your mentor is coming from and where they are going, as well as where they are leading you.

If you are looking for a guide you will want to check out www.rennyconsulting.com

Everyone Needs A Guide!

~*Becoming A Mentor*~

Chapter Eleven

Now that you have a mentor you are on your way to becoming a master. First off know you are not going to master anything in a week, month or year, it takes about 10 years to master anything, studies say that it takes 10,000 hours to master a skill. I guess now you understand why you don't disconnect from your mentor to early.

Now that we are clear that mastery is not an overnight happening let's move onto why we move to master a skill, trade or profession. I mentioned earlier that mastery satisfies the soul. No one is content with just being okay at something. Learning to master a skill opens doors. Everyone knows that when studying karate the goal is to move toward the black belt. This is the same in anything worth doing you want to be the best at it.

What serious ballerina wants to just be a ballerina? The goal is to be a prima ballerina. Tiger Woods did not just want to play golf he wanted to win the Masters. You see. If you are serious about your passion you should want to be a master at it. Yes it takes work and time but anything worth having does. You just have to make that commitment to your goal, your skill, in order to make sure you meet a level of mastery.

When becoming a master taking shortcuts that you have made up is a dangerous move. It only tacks on more time to your journey most times your shortcuts develops a bad habit that has to be unlearned before you move forward again. I like to ask my clients their goals and find out what they are moving to master. Then I like to find out the steps they have taken to get there. This allows me to see how much time they have already put into their goal and to see what steps were taken and which were skipped. Then I am able to work from there. I know their strengths and weaknesses and I can help them connect or reconnect with their goals.

If you desire to be an music artist I want to know how many songs you have written, how many you have recorded if any, how long have you been singing, have you had training are you being trained now? Are you seeing the point, in order to master singing you have to have been moving toward it somehow in some way? You don't just wake up one day and decide oh I am going to be a great singer. Sure you may have a real natural talent but that is only part of the puzzle. You need to learn to master that talent. Learn to sing in the recording studio, in stadiums, in small settings.

I remember when my husband started producing

music. He had the years of experience as an artist and in the business but producing was new; he thought he was just going to jump into it. I was so hard on him. I let him know I was not feeling the music he was making. That made him put in ridiculous hours to perfect the skill he and I both knew he had. After five years of unending persistence and more than 10,000 hours he began to move into a level of mastery. I could literally tell each time he was moving to another level. And yes he had a guide, he enrolled in one of the top placement firms, which critiques and advises producers on their submissions and he surrounded himself with other producers. This helped him see his music from outside of himself.

That reminds me of when I was in fashion design school one of my professors told me in the beginning that I would not make it through the program because I had a job and I needed those hours to work on my designs and skills. Well we know how I feel about someone telling me no or that I can't have something. I did make it through the program but I did have to let go of the job. I needed the hours, the same professor met me at the end and told me he didn't think I was going to pull it off but he pulled out of me the potential mastery he knew was there. He did what mentors are supposed to do.

You can master anything you set your mind to. You just have to find the drive and determination. Once determination kicks in you are on your way. Nothing will stop you. I have become that way about life. I am determined to be a master of my own destiny and a master of change. That is why I am sought after as a consultant. I have mastered change and the ability to create order. What are you mastering? What are you putting the time and effort into?

Whatever it is you desire to accomplish the ability for you to master it is there. Maybe you didn't realize before this that you wanted to master something or that you even could, but now you know and it is your time to go out there and put the time in. Make the time for your passion. Find the mentor that is going to push you to your master zone and soar to new levels that used to only exist in your imagination. Become the prima, the black belt, the master in your arena.

~New Beginnings~

Chapter Twelve

I want to thank you for believing in yourself and taking this journey with me. I know you are well on your way to being the success I know you are and that you see yourself being. Wash your hands of the past, because that is what it is, the past. You can't do anything with it so leave it where it is. Don't look back. Forgive yourself and the others that were players or characters in those seasons. You are starting fresh.

This is your new beginning. Don't let anything stop you. You are now a serious sower. You have your goals and you're your own boss. You know how to treat money. You are sitting under the right mentor and you are working toward mastery. You have even taken advantage of going to www.letusbringorder.com to start your membership and I see you getting really serious and I see you seeking more help at www.rennyconsulting.com. I know that sounds like a new you to me.

Relax and don't worry about the people you can't take along. The right friendship and relationship will show up all around you. You just need to be ready. I am excited for you. You are building a strong foundation and your hard work will pay off, and when I meet you at the top I will know we took this journey together and you were one of the willing students.

Remember, this will mean as much to you as you open up and allow yourself to receive. If you have read this looking to receive nothing then that is what you will walk away with. But if you read this book open to change and to have a chance to bring order, you will walk away with wealth beyond wealth. This book has shown you the keys to the palace and you will take them right to the doorway.

You will be the same one that seeks further knowledge and wealth. You will need to see more secrets, gain more revelation and I will be awaiting your return. For the teacher appears when the student is ready.

Your new beginning comes with a season of willingness to expand and learn. Your eyes have opened to the potential of more. To the possibility of a new life, order awaits you. You and your family will thank you for taking this journey. Understand that there is no turning back for you. You have opened a door that is inviting you in and once you walk in you will want to stay and find your way to the next door and you shall. You shall find the next door and begin to plan your way to the one after that. The joy you receive from meeting your goals will compel you to make a new set and start the journey once again.

This is your life and it is time you begin to live as if this is not about anything or anyone else. Others will benefit from your success but you will first have to focus on you to get you to the success.

Once again I thank you for loving yourself enough to start this change. May your life be filled with wealth, health and prosperity. See yourself as you want others to see you and dream big.

ABOUT THE AUTHOR

Verleiz Lattimore was born in New York, growing up with a well-rounded education and understanding of people. After several years of working for the Board of Education Verleiz found herself ready to break out of the box, following the devastation of losing her mother to cancer, which started an extreme chain of events leading to a spiritual transformation and growth. Mrs. Lattimore now is very active in ministry and counseling, while also working with her husband on their empire and creating their own destiny. To learn more about Verleiz please visit www.VerleizLattimore.com.

For more about Mrs. Lattimore and great resources go to www.letusbringorder.com

and

www.rennyconsulting.com

www.LetUsBringOrder.com

www.LetUsBringOrder.com

www.ingramcontent.com/pod-product-compliance
Lightning Source LLC
Chambersburg PA
CBHW072157090426

42740CB00012B/2302